ST. PATRICK'S DAY

by Charly Haley

Cody Koala

An Imprint of Pop!

popbooksonline.com

abdobooks.com
Published by Pop!, a division of ABDO, PO Box 398166, Minneapolis, Minnesota 55439. Copyright © 2019 by POP, LLC. International copyrights reserved in all countries. No part of this book may be reproduced in any form without written permission from the publisher. Pop!™ is a trademark and logo of POP, LLC.

Printed in the United States of America, North Mankato, Minnesota

082018
012019

THIS BOOK CONTAINS RECYCLED MATERIALS

Cover Photo: iStockphoto
Interior Photos: iStockphoto, 1, 5 (top), 9; Shutterstock Images, 5 (bottom left), 5 (bottom right), 7, 10, 13, 15, 16, 19, 20

Editor: Meg Gaertner
Series Designer: Laura Mitchell

Library of Congress Control Number: 2018949960
Publisher's Cataloging-in-Publication Data
Names: Haley, Charly, author.
Title: St. Patrick's day / by Charly Haley.
Description: Minneapolis, Minnesota : Pop!, 2019 | Series: Holidays | Includes online resources and index.
Identifiers: ISBN 9781532161995 (lib. bdg.) | ISBN 9781641855709 (pbk) | ISBN 9781532163050 (ebook)
Subjects: LCSH: St. Patrick's day--Juvenile literature. | Holidays--Juvenile literature.
Classification: DDC 394.262--dc23

Hello! My name is

Cody Koala

Pop open this book and you'll find QR codes like this one, loaded with information, so you can learn even more!

Scan this code* and others like it while you read, or visit the website below to make this book pop.

popbooksonline.com/st-patricks-day

*Scanning QR codes requires a web-enabled smart device with a QR code reader app and a camera.

Table of Contents

Chapter 1

St. Patrick's Day

People are wearing green.

They show **shamrocks**

and Irish flags. It is

St. Patrick's Day.

Watch a video here!

St. Patrick's Day is celebrated each year on March 17. It is a day to celebrate Irish **heritage**.

You do not need to be Irish to celebrate St. Patrick's Day.

March

Mon	Tue	Wed	Thu	Fri	Sat	Sun
						1
2	3	4	5	6	7	8
9	10	11	12	13	14	15
16	17	18	19	20	21	22
23	24	25	26	27	28	29
30	31					

Chapter 2

St. Patrick

Hundreds of years ago, a man named Patrick moved to Ireland. People believe he taught the **religion** of Christianity to Irish people.

Learn more here!

People were thankful for Patrick's teaching. He became known as St. Patrick. He died on March 17, 461. St. Patrick's Day is celebrated on the **anniversary** of his death.

Chapter 3

Irish Heritage

St. Patrick's Day began as a way to honor St. Patrick and his teachings. But the holiday has grown. Now it is a day to celebrate all Irish people.

Complete an activity here!

Many Irish people first came to the United States in the 1800s. At that time, many Irish Americans faced **discrimination**. People were mean to them.

Now Irish heritage is celebrated across the United States. St. Patrick's Day is popular in the United States and Ireland.

Irish people all over the world celebrate St. Patrick's Day.

Chapter 4

Celebrations

Many cities have big **parades** on St. Patrick's Day. People wear green. They eat Irish food. Some people even color their food green.

Learn more here!

People show shamrocks
and Irish flags on St. Patrick's
Day. They remember
St. Patrick.

St. Patrick was known
for using a shamrock
in his teachings.

Making Connections

Text-to-Self

Have you ever celebrated St. Patrick's Day?
How would you like to celebrate it?

Text-to-Text

Have you read any other books about holidays?
What did you learn?

Text-to-World

Have you ever been to a St. Patrick's Day parade?
What did you see and hear there?

Glossary

anniversary – recognition of a date on which something important happened.

discrimination – to treat someone unfairly because of how they look or where they are from.

heritage – personal history passed down through families and groups of people.

parade – a community event in which marching bands and other groups walk down a street and perform.

religion – a set of beliefs.

shamrock – a leaf that is divided into three parts.

Index

Online Resources

popbooksonline.com

Thanks for reading this Cody Koala book!

Scan this code* and others like it in this book, or visit the website below to make this book pop!

popbooksonline.com/st-patricks-day

*Scanning QR codes requires a web-enabled smart device with a QR code reader app and a camera.